The Evil & Danger of Neglecting the Souls of Men

THE EVIL
&
DANGER
OF NEGLECTING THE SOULS OF MEN

Philip Doddridge

The Evil and Danger of Neglecting the Souls of Men

Copyright © 2021 H&E Publishing
www.hesedandemet.com

Public Domain: Philip Doddridge, *The Evil and Danger of Neglecting the Souls of Men, Plainly and Seriously Represented*, in a Sermon Preach'd at A Meeting of Ministers at Kettering in Northamptonshire, October 15, 1741, and publish'd at their request by P. Doddridge, D.D. LONDON, Printed and sold by M. Fenner, at the Turks-Head in Grace-Church Street

Cover image: Struggle with the elements colors on canvas by hitforsa istock photo: 542013426

Project manager: Christopher Ellis Osterbrock

Paperback ISBN: 978-1-77484-036-8
Ebook ISBN: 978-1-77484-037-5

Contents

Introducing Philip Doddridge *Michael A.G. Haykin*	vii
Dedication	1
1. The Neglect of Souls	21
2. Excuses	37
3. Caution for Young Ministers	47
4. The Evils of Neglect	59
5. Applications and Practical Inferences	71
Scripture Index	79

Introducing Philip Doddridge

Michael A.G. Haykin

The Particular Baptist from the Midlands, William Carey (1761–1834), is often regarded as the pioneer voice in English-speaking circles for the urgent need to take the Gospel beyond the cultural horizons of western Europe. But it is very evident that Carey's iconic status in this regard has overshadowed earlier figures who had a similar passion. The author of the sermon that you hold in your hands was one such individual: Philip Doddridge (1702–1751). Doddridge is a tremendously important figure in the development of British Dissent in the eighteenth century, as it moved away from the somewhat insular world of late seventeenth-century Puritanism and became a key participant in the Evangelical revivals of the eighteenth century and the global expansion of Christianity.

Doddridge was the pastor of an Independent (Congregationalist) church at Castle Hill in Northampton from 1729 till his death. If he is remembered today, it is as a hymn-writer and as the author of a minor spiritual classic, *The Rise and Progress of Religion in the Soul* (1745), which played a key role in the conversion of William Wilberforce (1759–1833), among others. As Alan Everitt has noted, though, Doddridge's contribution to eighteenth-century Evangelicalism was substantial.[1] He was a leading figure in education, both of future pastors at his Dissenting Academy and also of children. Everitt is emphatic that he should be considered the founder of the Sunday School movement rather than Robert Raikes (1736–1811). He played a major role in the establishment of county hospitals for the poor and was an ardent champion of inoculation—his edit of David Some's *The Case for Receiving the Small-pox by Inoculation* (1750) was an important landmark in the fight against smallpox, the great killer of his day. He was a key link between Evangelical Anglican leaders of the revivals of this era like George Whitefield (1714–1770) and Dissenters like Isaac Watts (1674–1748). In fact, W.R. Ward has argued that Doddridge "was a Methodist in the sense of an adherent of

---

[1] Alan Everitt, "Springs of Sensibility: Philip Doddridge of Northampton and the Evangelical Tradition" in his *Landscapes and Community in England* (London: Bloomsbury, 1985), 211–212. I have found this study such an important essay that, according to my reckoning, I have read it through no less than four times in the past decade.

Introducing Philip Doddridge

the movement of revival and reform."[2] And he was an important voice for churches committing themselves to evangelism at home and overseas, as this sermon well reveals.

I do not think it was at all fortuitous that William Carey was baptized by John Ryland, Jr. (1753–1825) in 1783 in the River Nene, near the foot of the slope upon which Doddridge's Castle Hill Church stood. In those days a road led directly from the chapel to the brink of the river, a distance of around 200 yards. Nor was it fortuitous that Doddridge gave this sermon to a group of ministers at Kettering, seventeen miles or so north of Northampton, for it was at Kettering that the Baptist Missionary Society was formed fifty years later, in 1792 that sent Carey to India the following year. Is it mere romanticism to think that Doddridge's missions-minded mantle, so evident in this text, came to rest upon Carey? I trow not!

Further reading

In addition to Everitt's fine essay on Doddridge's piety, there are three important works on Doddridge that should

---

[2] W.R. Ward, *The Protestant Evangelical Awakening* (Cambridge: Cambridge University Press, 1992), 348.

be mentioned as the best place to begin further exploration of Doddridge's life and legacy. The first two are biographical studies: Malcolm Deacon, *Philip Doddridge of Northampton 1702–52* (Northampton: Northamptonshire Libraries, 1980) and Alan C. Clifford, *The Good Doctor, Philip Doddridge of Northampton: A Tercentenary Tribute* (Norwich: Charenton Reformed Publishing, 2002). Then, there is the excellent study of Doddridge's thought by Robert Strivens, *Philip Doddridge and the Shaping of Evangelical Dissent* (2015, London; New York: Routledge, 2016). Alongside these three valuable studies, there are two collections of essays that merit mention: Geoffrey F, Nuttall, ed., *Philip Doddridge, 1702–51: His Contribution to English Religion* (London: Independent Press, 1951) and R.L. Greenall, ed., *Philip Doddridge, Nonconformity and Northampton* (Leicester: Department of Adult Education, University of Leicester, 1981), which contains an earlier version of Everitt's essay.

Dedication

*To the associated Protestant Dissenting ministers
in the Counties of Norfolk and Suffolk.
Particularly, those with whom the author had an interview at
Denton, June the 30, 1741*

Gentlemen, my reverend fathers and brethren, and much esteemed friends,

The condescending respect and endeared affection with which you were pleased to receive me in my late visit to your parts, and the very great satisfaction which I found in your company at Denton and elsewhere, have left a very delightful memorial on my heart, and have impressed those unfeigned sentiments of gratitude and esteem which it would be painful to suppress. Most gladly therefore do I take this method, in a few words, publicly to avow them, and I sincerely congratulate the happy societies, respectively under your care, who statedly enjoy the benefit of those valuable labours—a little taste of which gave me an exquisite pleasure beyond what it is possible for me to fully express.

NEGLECTING THE SOULS OF MEN

Nevertheless, desirous as I am of erecting some little monument of thankful friendship, I should not have attempted it by inscribing this plain sermon to you; unless the subject of it had been such as peculiarly suited your perusal; and, if I may be permitted to say it, amidst all its imperfections, your patronage too.

No doubt, many of you gentlemen remember that after the public worship at Denton was over, on that memorable day which I shall always remember among the most delightful of my whole life, toward the evening you were pleased to indulge me in the liberty of a private conference. In this conference I said before you some hints of a scheme which I was then forming for the revival of religion in our parts. A scheme which you were pleased in the general to approve, and in several particulars to ripen by your prudent and valuable counsels.

Greatly encouraged by the sanction which your concurrence gave to the plan; and also, by that which it received from the approbation of some of the most eminent of the London ministers of different denominations to whom I had an opportunity of communicating it on my return home. I proposed it in general to my reverend and worthy brethren in these parts, at a meeting of ministers which was held here at Northampton, about the middle of August. The

Dedication

proposals were, in the general, very well received and it was agreed to take them into a more particular consideration in a conference at our next assembly, to be held at Kettering, on Thursday, the 15th of October.

To that conference, gentlemen, the sermon with which I now present you was introductory, and the result of it was that the heads of the scheme I had concerted with you at Denton with a few other particulars, which had not then occurred to my thoughts, were unanimously approved, and we are taking proper measures for carrying them into execution. And, as this discourse may fall into the hands of some who may be curious to know what the particulars were—and as I bore them so frequently in my thoughts through many passages of my sermon—I shall take the freedom here to give an account of them, though, I doubt not, but the most material of them are fresh in your memories.

Queries considered

It seemed most agreeable to the deference due to the reverend assembly, to propose the scheme in the form of queries, on which the following resolutions were formed, *nemine contradicente*.[3]

---

[3] *Nemine contradicente* meaning not comparable; with nobody contradicting; without dissent.

Neglecting the Souls of Men

1. That it may tend to the advancement of religion, that the ministers of this association, if they have not very lately done it, should agree to preach one Lord's Day on family religion and another on secret prayer; and that the time should be fixed, in humble hope that concurrent labours, connected with concurrent petitions to the throne of grace, might produce some happy effect.

2. That it is proper, that pastoral visiting should be more solemnly attended to and that greater care should be taken in personal inspection than has generally been used. And that it may be conducive to this good end that each minister should take an exact survey of his flock. And that he note down the names of the heads of families, the children, the servants, and other single persons in his auditory in order to keep proper memorandums concerning each. That he may judge the better of the particulars of his duty regarding everyone, and may observe how his visits, exhortations, and admonitions, correspond to their respective characters and circumstances.

3. That consequent on this survey, it will be proper, as soon as possible and henceforward at least once a year, to visit, if it be practicable, every head of a family under our ministerial care, with a solemn charge to attend to the business of religion in their hearts, and houses, watching over

Dedication

their domestics in the fear of the Lord. We, at the same time, professing our readiness to give them all proper assistances for this purpose.

4. That it will be highly expedient, immediately, or as soon as may be, to set up the work of catechizing in one form or another, and to keep to it statedly for one half of the year at least. And that it is probable, future counsels may ripen some scheme for carrying on this work in a manner which may tend greatly to the propagation of real, vital, catholic Christianity, in the rising generation.

5. That there is reason to apprehend, there are, in all our congregations, some pious and valuable persons who live in a culpable neglect of the Lord's Supper. And it is our duty, particularly to inform ourselves who they are and to endeavor, by our prayers to God and our serious addresses to them, to introduce them into communion (to which, I question not, we shall all willingly add), cautiously guarding against anything in the methods of admission, which may justly discourage sincere Christians of a tender and timorous temper.

6. That it is to be feared, there are some, in several of our communions at least, who behave in such a manner as to give just offence, and that we may be in great danger of making ourselves partakers of other men's sins if we do not

animadvert upon them. And if they will not reform, or if the crime be notorious, we ought, in duty to God, to them, and to all around us, solemnly to cut them off from our sacramental communion as a reproach to the church of Christ.

7. That it may on many accounts be proper to advise our people to enter into little bands, or societies, for religious discourse and prayer; each consisting of six or eight, to meet for these good purposes once a week, or a fortnight, as may best with their other engagements and affairs.

8. That it might be advisable, if it can be done, to select out of each congregation under our care, a small number of persons, remarkable for experienced prudence, seriousness, humility and zeal, to act as a stated council for promoting religion in the said society. And that it would be proper they should have some certain times of meeting with each other and with the minister, to join their counsels, and their prayers for the public good.

9. That so far as we can judge, it might, by the divine blessing, conduce to the advancement of these valuable ends, that neighbouring ministers, in one part of our land and another (especially in this country) should enter in associations, to strengthen the hands of each other by united consultations and prayer. And that meetings of ministers might, by some obvious regulations, be made more

Dedication

extensively useful than they often are. In which view it was farther proposed (with unanimous approbation), that these meetings should be held at certain periodical times; that each member of the association should endeavor (if possible) to be present, studying to order his affairs so as to guard against unnecessary hindrances; that public worship should begin and end sooner than it commonly has done on these occasions; that each pastor preach at these assemblies in his turn; that the minister of the place determine who shall be employed in prayer; that after a moderate repast, to be managed with as little trouble and expense as may be, an hour or two in the afternoon be spent in religious conference and prayer, and in taking into consideration (merely as a friendly council and without the least pretense to any right of authoritative decision), the concerns of any brother or any society, which may be brought before us for our advice; and finally, that every member of this association shall consider it as an additional obligation upon him, to endeavor to be, so far as he justly and honourably can, a friend and guardian to the reputation, comfort, and usefulness of all his brethren in the Christian ministry, near or remote, of whatever party and denomination.

10. That it may be proper to enter into some farther measures, to regulate the admission of young persons into

the ministry—the particulars here were referred to farther consideration, but so far as I can judge, the plan proposed will be pretty nearly this: that if any student within the compass of this association desires to be admitted as a preacher, he apply to the ministers at one of their periodical meetings. When, if they be in the general satisfied that he is a person of a fair character, in sacramental communion with a Christian society, and one who has gone through a regular course of preparatory studies, they will appoint three of their number to examine more particularly into his acquaintance with, and sense of the great doctrines of Christianity as delivered in the Scripture, and into the progress he has made in literature, the views with which he professes to undertake the ministry, and in general, his aptness to teach. In order to judging of which, it may be proper that a theological thesis be exhibited in Latin, and a popular sermon composed by the candidate, be submitted to the perusal of the examiners; that if they, in their consciences, believe he is fit to be employed in the Christian ministry, they give him a certificate of that approbation, which he may be desired to produce at the next general meeting, that his testimonials may be signed by all the associated ministers present, and he solemnly recommended to God by prayer.

Dedication

Thus, gentlemen, you have a view of the scheme as it now lies before us, and as every article except the last (not yet considered among us) was approved at Kettering at the time above-mentioned. I will take leave to add one particular more, which has since occurred to my thoughts, and which I here submit to your consideration, and to that of my other reverend brethren into whose hands this may fall, especially those of our own association.

11. Question whether something might not be done in most of our congregations towards assisting in the propagation of Christianity abroad, and spreading it in some of the darker parts of our own land? In pursuance of which it is further proposed that we endeavor to engage as many pious people of our respective congregations as we can, to enter themselves into a society in which the members may engage themselves to some peculiar cares, assemblies, and contributions, with a regard to this great end. I will not swell this dedication with the particulars of that scheme, which has been formed to his purpose, but rather choose an insert at the bottom of the page a copy of such an association which I am endeavouring to introduce among my own people, and which several have already signed.

Resolutions affirmed

It is a feeble essay; and the effects of it in one congregation can be but very small, but, if it were generally to be followed, who can tell what a harvest such a little grain might at length produce? May God multiply it a thousand-fold![4]

    I. That we purpose, as God shall enable us, to be daily putting up some earnest petitions to the throne of grace, for the advancement of the gospel in the world, and for the success of all the faithful servants of Christ, who are engaged in the work of it, especially among the heathen nations.

    II. That we will assemble at least four times a year in our place of public worship, at such seasons as shall by mutual consent to be appointed, to spend some time in solemn prayer together on this important account. We hereby engage that we will, each of us, if we conveniently can, attend at such meetings, unless such circumstances happen as to lead us in our own consciences to conclude that it will be more acceptable in the sight of God that we should be employed in some other business elsewhere.

---

[4] We whose names are subscribed, being moved, as we hope and trust, by a real concern for the propagation of the kingdom of Christ in the world, have determined to form ourselves into a society for that end, on the following terms.

Dedication

III. We do hereby express our desire that some time may be then spent, if God give an opportunity, in reviewing those promises of Scripture that relate to the establishment of our redeemer's kingdom in the world; that our faith may be supported, and our prayers quickened by the contemplation of them.

IV. It is also our desire that whatever important information relating to the progress of the gospel be received from the various parts of this kingdom, or from foreign lands by any members of the society, they may be communicated to us at our general quarterly meetings; and the rest of us make it our request of our minister, that he will, where he can with convenience do it, keep up such correspondences; that we may be more capable of judging how far God answers our prayers, and those of his other servants, in this regard.

V. We further engage that, on these days of general meeting, every one of us will, as God shall be pleased to prosper us, contribute something; be it ever so little towards the carrying on of this pious design, which shall be lodged in the hands of a treasurer, to be chosen at the first meeting to be disposed of by him, and four other trustees, then also to be appointed, in such a manner as they shall judge most convenient towards supporting the expense of sending millionaires abroad; printing Bibles, or other useful books in foreign languages, establishing schools for the instruction of the ignorant, and the like.

VI. That the pastor for the time being, if one of the Society, be always one of those trustees, and that four more be annually nominated by the society at the first meeting after New-Years-Day with a power of choosing their treasurer out of their own number; and that the accounts of the former year be then laid before the society, or before a committee appointed to examine them.

VII. That members after the first meeting be admitted by the consent of the majority of the society present at some stated meeting; and that if any member think fit to withdraw, he signifies that purpose to the society, or to one of the trustees.

VIII. That brief minutes be taken at every meeting of the business dispatched, the persons admitted, the contributions made at it, &c.

To these rules we subscribe our hands, heartily praying that God may quicken us and many others by our means, to greater zeal in this, and in every good word and work. And that, joining in spirit with all those who in one place or another are devoting their lives to the advancement of the gospels, we may another day partake of their joy.

Dedication

A charge to diligence

Excuse me, my reverend and dear brethren, that I have detained you so long with these various particulars and permit me to conclude this address with beseeching you to join with me in humble prayer to him who knows the sincere regard to the temporal and eternal happiness of his creatures, by which the plain things of this dedication and sermon are dictated, that he may honour both with his blessing. If any parts of the scheme here laid before you have not indeed that subserviency to the great end proposed, which they are imagined to have, it would be a peculiar pleasure to me to be better informed. Yet I must take the liberty to say those must be strong arguments, which will prevail against the experience of the happy effects, that have for some time in my own congregation attended those, alas, too imperfect attempts, that I have made to carry them into execution. But if they are, as I assuredly believe, calculated to revive the languishing interest of real religion, may your advice, my honoured friends, in concurrence with that of my worthy brethren in these parts, and with the serious expostulations contained in the ensuing discourse, prevail on others to make the trial of them, which surely they will not repent in the nearest views of eternity.

Neglecting the Souls of Men

I persuade myself, gentlemen, that in the midst of these various cares and labours for the public service, to which, weak as I am, divine providence has called me, you will sometimes be repeating for me those suitable and pathetic petitions, which you were pleased, at Denton and elsewhere during my late interviews with you, to offer on my account. Petitions, which I never recollect without a most sensible pleasure, and by the very remembrance of which I find myself animated to this very day.

On my part, dear brethren, be assured of all the most affectionate good wishes, which sincere esteem, and grateful friendship can inspire. May that spirit of grace and supplication, the happy effects of which I so delightfully observed in those of you, on whom I had then an opportunity of attending, be in a still richer abundance poured forth upon you all! May you open your mouths boldly to declare the mysteries of God, as faithful witnesses to the truth and purity of his gospel, in the midst of a degenerate and back-sliding age. May you teach, not only publicly, but from house to house. May a truly primitive and scriptural discipline, which it is our privilege, that amidst all our discouragements we are able, not only to pray for, but to exercise, be impartially maintained. And in consequence of all this, may you have the pleasure to see your assemblies flourishing.

Dedication

May you feel your hearts daily cheered and animated by the visible success of your labours, and may there be no contention among you, unless it be who shall exert himself with the most exemplary prudence, zeal, and love, in the prosecution of so good a work. May each of you, in the sphere which providence has assigned him, be a burning and a shining light. And may the luster of your servant and active piety awaken (if any of them slumber), our brethren of the established clergy, to guard against that growth of the dissenting interest, which must otherwise be the probable consequence of such measures. May they all emulate the most faithful and zealous among us, in the purity of their doctrine, in the seriousness and spirituality of their address, in the vigilance of their pastoral inspection, in their tender care to train up the rising generation for God, and above all, in the distinguished sanctity of their lives.

This will unite our hearts in such mutual esteem and affection, that even while in different communions, we shall treat each other like brethren and friends and fellow-labourers in the vineyard of Christ; far more endeared by our common love to our divine master, and the souls he has redeemed, than alienated by our different apprehensions, as to the particular mode by which that interest is to be promoted. The question between us will not then be, "How much may we lawfully impose?" and "How much may we lawfully dispute?" But on the one side, it will be enquired, "What may we wave?" And on the other, "What may we acquiesce in, from a principle of mutual tenderness and respect, without displeasing our common Lord and injuring that great cause of original Christianity, which he has appointed us to guard?" Thus, may the flames of undissembled love purge away our dross, and cement us into one mass, where the union will be the closer in proportion to the degree in which the metal is the nobler and the more refined. And thus, may it cause those fetters to fall off under the weight and the straightness of which, however they may have been gilded over, the worthiest persons that wear them must secretly groan.

We are praying and waiting for that happy day, which, whenever it appears, will be the glorious earnest of the revival of the Protestant and the Christian cause. In the meantime, may each of us have a pleasing consciousness that we are laboring to promote it, or at least that while we are waiting for the appearance of the great physician among us, we do not, by our own rashness, exasperate those distempers, which in his absence we cannot heal! A wish and a care, in which, I am sure, you will concur with,

Dedication

Gentlemen,
Your most affectionate brother,
and faithful and obliged
humble servant,

Philipp Doddridge
Northampton
February 1, 1741–1742.

The Evil & Danger
of Neglecting the Souls of Men

"If you forbear to deliver them that are drawn to death, and those that are ready to be slain: If you say, behold, we knew it not: Doth not he that pondereth the heart, consider it? and he that keepeth thy soul, doth not he know it? and shall not he render to every man according to his works?"
Proverbs 24:11–12

1
The Neglect of Souls

The interviews of the ministers of Christ will always be pleasant in proportion to the degree in which they are animated by divine grace to think and act worthy of their honourable relation to him and to each other. We in these parts have great reason for thankfulness, that we have so long known, by happy experience, how good and how pleasant for brethren to dwell together in unity (Ps. 133:1), and it is with peculiar joy that I reflect. We are met this day, not only to express and cultivate our mutual affection, but also by our united counsels, to strengthen each other's hands in the work of our God, and to concert measures for the more effectual revival of religion in the several places where providence has especially assigned it to our stated care. As iron sharpens iron, so a man often sharpens the countenance of his friend (Prov. 27:17). Since I am called to address you, this day, on so solemn and important an occasion, most gladly would I contribute my utmost to whet your spirits and my own. To awaken us all to that zeal for the service of our common master, which will render the various duties of our office abundantly delightful and our reward in heaven proportionably great. Oh, that what I have now to say might be like goads to penetrate all our minds, and like nails, securely fastened in our memories and our hearts, given forth from the one great shepherd (Eccl. 12:11). May all the instruments with which he is furnishing us in our pastoral work, be wisely and faithfully employed; and may the masters of assemblies this day be excited to use them with great skill and diligence in his service!

And as for you, my brethren in more private stations of life, I persuade myself you will hear me patiently and candidly. For though but little of my discourse will be immediately addressed to you, it is your cause I shall be pleading in the whole of it. You will therefore, I hope, be often lifting up your hearts to God for the success of it—and will also be considering what intimations of your own duty you may collect from what I am to address to those of a more public character. For though the words of my text may, with peculiar propriety, be applied to the ministers of the gospel, they were at first spoken with a much more general view; nor is there one soul in the assembly who may not consider them as directed by God to him, as truly as if his own name were prefixed to them. If you forbear to deliver them that are drawn to death, and those that are ready to be slain; if you

Neglect of Souls

say, or (as it might be rendered[5]), though you may say, "behold we know it not: Doth not he that pondereth the heart, consider it? and he that keepeth thy soul, doth not he know it? and will not he render to every man according to his works?"[6]

For the explication of which words, with all becoming deference to the superior judgment of some before whom I speak, I would offer these three plain and obvious remarks.

The neglect of souls is criminal

The omission, which is here charged as so displeasing to God, though immediately referring to men's natural lives, must surely imply that the neglect of their souls is much more criminal.

The test strongly implies that we shall be exposed to guilt and condemnation before God, by forbearing to deliver them that are drawn to death and those that are ready to be slain. This must directly refer to innocent persons brought into visible and extreme danger by some oppressive enemy,

---

[5] It is well known, that the particle "כִּי" often signifies *although*. Thus our translators very justly render it several places: See Exodus 13:17; Joshua 17:18; 2 Samuel 23:5; Ezekiel 11:16; and Habakkuk 3:17. And if they had done so in several others, they would have expressed the sense and connection of the original much more plainly. Compare Genesis 8:21; Psalm 14:6; 25:11; Isaiah 38:18–19.

[6] Proverbs 24:12.

either by the sudden assault of a private person, or by some unjust prosecution under forms of law; and may particularly extend to cases where we have reason to believe a capital sentence has been passed in consequence of false witness, detected before execution is done.[7] When cases of one sort or the other occur, we may consider Solomon as requiring just as his father David had done, that we should, by such interpositions as suit the case in question, and that station in which providence has fixed us, defend the poor and the fatherless, or those who are oppressed as orphans often are. We should do justice to the afflicted and the needy, and to rid them out of the hand of the wicked (Ps. 82:2-4). And though this may expose us to popular clamours, we should adopt the heroic resolution of Job—not fearing a great multitude, nor permitting the reproach of families to terrify us, so as to keep silence and not go out of the door (Job 31:34). One would hope such attacks as these seldom happened under the peaceful and equitable reign of Solomon. But as violence and fraud are in some degree the product of all

---

[7] It was allowed among the Jews that if any person could offer anything in favour of a prisoner, after sentence was passed, he might be heard before execution was done: And therefore it was usual (as the Mishnah shows) that when a man was led to execution, a crier went before him and proclaimed, "This man is now going to be executed for such a crime and such and such are witnesses against him; whoever knows him to be innocent, let him come forth and make it appear."

climates and ages, he had, no doubt, in some instances observed them[8] and had remarked a culpable negligence in those who ought to have interposed to have delivered the victims from such an undeserved stroke. On which account, he judged it necessary to enter his solemn protest against an indolence and cowardice so detrimental to society, and so offensive to God, the great guardian of it.

Now you will be pleased to observe that delivering persons reduced to such extreme danger in the circumstance I have described would generally be an act of charity attended with great danger, or with great trouble. And if the neglect of that be (as you see it is) represented as highly criminal, it must be a much greater offence to suffer any to perish, for want of either food, shelter, or harbour, in circumstances where person is able, by a little trouble, expense, or care, to preserve their lives. We may argue by a consequence yet stronger than this: it must be a much more heinous crime than neglecting worldly goods that, by our neglect, we

---

[8] It appears by several hints in Solomon's writings, that the gay, expensive, and luxurious manner of living, which (though directly contrary to the genius of the Jewish religion) was introduced in his days, had its natural effect in producing frequent thefts, perjuries, robberies, and murders, and, worst of all, abominable corruption among magistrates, and great iniquity in judicial affairs. Compare Proverbs 1:10-19; 3:29; 4:16-17; 6:12-14; 12:5-6; 17:15; 18:5; 21:7, 28; 22:22-23; 23:10-11, 20-21; 24:15, 23; 28:15, 17, 20-21; 29:4, 10; Ecclesiastes 3:16-17; 4:1-2, 8.

permit the ruin of men's souls without endeavouring their recovery, when they are drawn away to the extremist danger of eternal death, and are ready to be slain by the sword of divine justice. For if temporal life should be thus tenderly regarded, and expense or danger should be cheerfully met in the defense of it, judge you, sirs, as in the fight of God how much more precious the redemption of the soul is, which will soon cease, even forever (Ps. 49:8).

Nay, I might go yet farther and draw an inference, if it were necessary, from that humane and charitable precept of the Jewish legislator (Exod. 23:4–5): "If you meet your enemy's ox or his ass going astray, you shall surely bring it back again to him again. If you see the ass of him that hates you, lying under his burthen, will you forbear, or (as it might be rendered) would you refrain, to help him?" Or could you be so cruel as to harbor a thought of it? No, you shall surely help with him. See, you shall go, if it be necessary, and join your strength with that of your enemy, to raise the beast from the ground.

Now if God not only regards the natural life of a man, but if he thus appears to care for oxen and asses, how much more must he require us to reduce wandering souls, and to do what we can to raise them, when pressed under the burthen of sin and in danger of being crushed into eternal misery?

Excuses

The text seems to suppose that men would be ready to excuse themselves for this neglect.

It is true that at the first sight of a miserable object we naturally find a strong impulse to endeavor to relieve it. Our hearts do, as it were, spring in our bosoms and urge us forward to exert ourselves on such an occasion. This seems to be intimated by that word, which we render "forbear," which often signifies to check, restrain, and hold back a person from what he is eager on doing.[9] But the wise man intimates there may be danger of suppressing these generous allies of the soul on the first view of the object, of suffering our charity to cool, and then of searching out apologies for our inactivity. You may be ready to say, "Behold, we know it not."

---

[9] The same word, in original Hebrew, is used to express the restraint put on the passion of Abimelech for Sarah (Genesis 20:6), on the revenge of David when insulted by Nabal (1 Samuel 25:39), and on the martial fury of David's party when pursuing the rebels under Absalom (2 Samuel 18:16). Compare Job 16:6 and Proverbs 21:26.

Neglecting the Souls of Men

I did not particularly see the danger; I did not, however, apprehend it to be so extreme. Or I did not know the innocence of the person in danger; or if I did believe it, I knew not how to deliver him. I did not think the interposition of such a person as I, could be of any importance in such an affair. I was sorry to see innocence overborn, and weakness oppressed; but I was myself too weak to contend with the mightier oppressor; too poor, too ignorant, or too busy, to meddle in an affair, where those who were much my superiors were concerned, and had determined the case. I had no obligations to the person in danger. I had no concern with him, nor anything to do to embarrass myself with his affairs.

If these excuses be just, it is well. God requires impossibilities from no man; nor does he expect that persons should rashly throw themselves upon difficulties and dangers when there is no such rational prospect of doing good, as may balance the hazard.

Excuses over-ruled

Nevertheless the text supposes that these excuses might often be over-ruled by an appeal to men's consciences as in the sight of God.

Neglect of Souls

Does not he that ponders the heart consider it, and he that keeps your soul, does he know it? As if he should have said,

> It is an easy thing to excuse omissions, so that a fellow-creature shall have nothing to reply, but whoever you are that reads these words, I charge you to remember that it is comparatively a very little matter to be judged of man's judgment, he that judges you is the Lord (1 Cor. 4:3-4). The Lord ponders the heart: he weighs, in a most accurate balance, all its most secret sentiments. I therefore cut off all chicane and trifling debate at once, by placing you in his presence and laying open your conscience there. You can't answer me; but can you not answer the heart-searching God? Does not he, the great father of spirits, see in every instance how inferior spirits conduct themselves? Does he not precisely know the situation in which your heart was at the very moment in question? You say, "you knew it not," but he is witness, whether you indeed did or did not know it. And he also sees all the opportunities and advantages, which you had for knowing it—all the hints, which might have been traced out, to open a more explicit and particular knowledge—every glimpse which you had when you were (like the priest, when he spied at a distance the wounded traveler) passing by on the other

side (Luke 10:31), and perhaps affecting to look the contrary way.

Nor was it in vain that the wise man renewed his expostulation in a different form. He that keeps your soul, does he not know it? As if he had said,

Consider God, as keeping your own soul. As holding it in life (Ps. 66:9). As preserving your Spirit by his continued visitation (Job 10:12). Then say, "Oh you that neglects the life of your brother, whether he must not be highly displeased with that neglect?" May he not reasonably expect that while he, the Lord of heaven and earth, condescends to become your guardian, you should learn of him and be, according to your ability and in your sphere, a guardian to the whole human race. That you should endeavor, in every instance, to ward off danger from the life, from the soul of your brother?

And that these thoughts may enter into the mind with all their weight, it is added once more, in this pointed form of interrogation; will not he render to every man according to his works?

NEGLECT OF SOULS

I appeal to your own heart, is he not a being of infinite moral, as well as natural, perfections? Will he not, as the Judge of all the earth, do right (Gen. 18:25)? Would he not have remembered, and rewarded, your generous care for the preservation of the miserable creature in question? And, on the other hand, will he not reckon with you for such a failure? Human laws, indeed, cannot punish such neglects, but the supreme legislator can and will do it. Think of these things, and guard against such fatal negligence in every future instance: Think of them, and humble yourself deeply before God, for every past instance, in which such guilt has been incurred.

You easily perceive, from this explication of my text, that (as I hinted above) I might very properly make it the foundation of a discourse "on the care of souls in general," addressed to persons of all ranks and professions in life; especially to parents, and masters, and heads of families.[10] And they will indeed have an evident share in what I am to say, and therefore I would bespeak their particular attention to it. But considering the occasion of our present assembly, and also considering how much of their fidelity in the

---

[10] I have argued the matter at large with them in my *Sermons on Education*, which, if God permit, will shortly be reprinted with an appendix. See *Sermons on the Religious Education of Children* (London: Samuel Hall, 1794).

performance of their duty will probably, under God, depend upon the exhortations, instructions, and assistances they receive from us, I shall chiefly address these things to you, my reverend fathers and brothers in the ministry, and intreat your patient and candid attendance, while I speak to you with all possible plainness and seriousness, as in the name and presence of our common master.

To faithful ministers

God is my witness that I mean not to insinuate the least disrespectful thought with regard to any one of you. Indeed, I have not the least temptation to it. For I can say, with equal integrity and pleasure, that I believe few of your profession in the Christian world (glorious as that profession is, and happy as it is in many that adorn it), are more constant, more upright, or more zealous, in the course of their public ministry. I repeat it with great cheerfulness that I am inwardly persuaded that few of the servants of Christ are, or in any modern age have been, more faithfully solicitous to declare to their people the whole counsel of God; or to enforce their public exhortations by the silent but powerful eloquence of a blameless, holy, and exemplary life. And of this, I assuredly believe you have a testimony in the consciences of all around you, and even of multitudes who are

Neglect of Souls

not the stated attendants on your labours; and who perhaps, in such a case, are under some temptations to err on the severe, rather than on the candid extreme. So that in this respect I could cheerfully say, would to God, that all your brethren in the Christian ministry, throughout the nation, and the world were even as you. Nevertheless, permit me to say it without offence (for I say it in the fear of God, and with the sincerest deference and friendship to you), I am afraid the extensive and important obligations of the ministerial office are not generally considered and remembered among us as they ought. I apprehend much more might be done for the honour of God and the good of souls than is commonly done, I will not say, by those careless and profane wretches, who undertake the tremendous charge merely for the sake of worldly emoluments. More might be done by those who the plainness of prophetic language call dumb dogs that cannot bark and greedy dogs that can never have enough (Isa. 56:10–11). Even by those who in the main have a principle of true religion in their hearts, who keep up the exercise of public worship in a regular and honourable manner, and appear not only irreproachable in their conversation, but, if considered as in private life, bringing forth the fruits of righteousness. I fear the learned, the wise, the virtuous, the pious minister is often negligent of a considerable part of his trust and charge and thereby fails to deliver, as he might, those that are drawn unto death, and perhaps are just ready to be slain. To awaken our spirits therefore from that insensibility in this respect into which they are so ready to fall, and so to improve the present opportunity, that the man of God may be perfect (2 Tim. 3:17), and thoroughly furnished to every good work which our office requires, I shall take the liberty,

I. Briefly to consider what excuses we may be most ready to offer for neglecting the souls of men.

II. Seriously to represent the great evil of that neglect in the sight of God, notwithstanding all those excuses. After which,

III. I shall add a few hints by way of reflection, as the time may admit.

And if a consciousness of my own past neglects, and an ignorance of circumstances in the congregations of my brethren, lead me to suppose some deficiencies greater than they really are, with regard to some that hear me, I hope they will forgive me this involuntary wrong. And likewise forgive me of those cautions which your own diligence and zeal render unnecessary. I am far from the thought of charging any particular person, and ground most of the remarks I now present on what is obvious in the temper of mankind,

Neglect of Souls

and on those infirmities of human nature to which the best of men are obnoxious. However by divine grace they may be conquered in a few of the most eminent for fidelity and zeal. I am to consider what excuses we may be ready to make for neglecting to do our utmost for the salvation of men's souls.

2
Excuses

Now I imagine one of the first thoughts that may present itself to our view upon such an occasion may be this:

Do something considerable for the invigorating of souls
Particularly, that we take care for their instruction in public; reading the Word of God to them when they are assembled together in his house, explaining and enforcing it in our expositions and sermons, presenting prayers and praises to God in their name, and, at proper seasons, administering the sacraments in such a manner as we judge most agreeable to the institution of our Lord Jesus Christ.

And so far indeed, it is well. A most wise and gracious constitution of our blessed redeemer it is that such ordinances should be administered on Solemn Stated Days[11] and by men appropriated to that employment. In consequence of which such knowledge is dispersed, as may be and undoubtedly is, through the divine blessing effectual for the salvation of many souls, so that ministers cannot go

---

[11] Specific dates upon a liturgical calendar designated for particular methods for worship.

through the external and public services of their function without giving their hearers some great and valuable advantages far beyond what the professors of any other religion can find in the rites of their various, and generally absurd, and superstitious worship. And I am not afraid to say, that this would make the Christian ministry, even in the hands of ignorant, careless, and vicious men, a blessing to the nation where it is settled, so long as reading the Scriptures, and almost any kind of prayers in an intelligible language make a part of divine service in their assemblies. Much more then will it be so in the hands of wise, sober, and religious men, though, through human frailty, they are much less zealous and active than it were to be wished they were, or than they ought to be.

But while we are thus pleading our diligence and care of the administration of public ordinances, it will be kindness to ourselves seriously to ask our own hearts, at least, how they are administered. It is (as I have elsewhere hinted) a very important trust to have the management of men's religious hours committed to us; their seasons of social worship being, comparatively, so short, and so infinitely momentous. I think we do almost, as it were, put our own lives in our hand while we undertake it and may justly tremble on the view of that awful account which we are to give for it.

Excuses

Mature consideration

I hope, sirs, we have the testimony of our own consciences before God, that we do not, on these solemn occasions, content ourselves with cold essays on here moral subjects, however acute, philosophical, or polite. Nor make it our main business in our sermons to seek the ornament and elegance of words, the refinements of criticism, or the nice arrangement of various complex and abstruse argumentations. When we speak in the name and presence of God to immortal creatures on the borders of eternity, I hope we entertain our hearers with plain, serious, and lively discourses on the most important doctrines of Christianity. I hope we speak of these doctrines in their due connection, and their relation to each other, in such a manner, as we, on mature consideration, do verily believe may have the most effectual tendency to bring them to God through Christ, and to produce and promote in their hearts, through the divine blessing, the great work of regeneration and holiness.

I hope and trust that, God is our witness and that the people of our charge are witnesses, not one of those who diligently attend our ministry, even if they were to miss a few succeeding Sabbaths, can fail to learn the way of salvation as exhibited in the gospel. I hope and trust that we speak of it as those that are in earnest and, from our very souls, do desire to answer the great ends of our ministry, in the prosperity of the redeemer's kingdom and the eternal happiness of those invaluable souls whom he has committed to our care. Otherwise we may incur great and fatal guilt, though public worship be constantly, decently carried on, and though a reasonable proportion of time be employed in it with numerous and attentive types of sounds.[12] To whom we may be as the lovely song of one that has a pleasant voice (Ezek. 33:32), while in the ears of God, for want of that fervent charity which should dictate and animate all, we are but as sounding brass or as a tinkling cymbal (1 Cor. 13:1).

But granting, as I would willingly suppose, and as with relation to you, my brethren, I do firmly believe all these reflections can be answered to satisfaction. Here is indeed a part of your duty honourably performed, and an important part of it too. But is that part, though ever so important, to be substituted for the whole? The diligent inspection of our flock, pastoral visits, the observation of the religious state of families, personal exhortations, admonitions, and cautions, by word or letter as prudence shall direct, the catechizing children, the promoting religious associations among the younger and the elder people of our charge, and the strict

---

[12] Auditories.

and resolute exercise of discipline in the several churches over which we preside are these no parts of our office? Will we say it with our dying breath, will we maintain it before the tribunal of Christ, that they did not belong to the Christian ministry? And if not, will our care in other parts of it be allowed as a sufficient excuse before him for our total omission of these? We have preached, prayed, and administered the sacraments. These things we should indeed have done, and when we had taken the care of congregations upon us, we could hardly avoid it, but surely our own consciences will now, or hereafter, tell us that we ought not to have left the others undone (Matt. 23:23).

Learn the responsibility of domestic worship
Consider that the care of particular persons more properly belongs to others and especially to heads of families, who have more opportunities of being serviceable to those under their charge, and indeed have the most immediate concern in them.

It certainly does. But does it belong to them alone? Or if it did, do not they belong to us and to our care? And is it not the part of every superior officer of a society to see to it that the subaltern officers be careful and diligent in the discharge of their duty? And in this case, are we to take it for granted that in our respective congregations, heads of families are of course so? That they pray in their families, and they read the scriptures, and other good books there, especially on the evening of the Lord's Day? That they catechize their children and solemnly press upon them, and upon their servants, the serious care of practical religion? Are we roundly to conclude without any further enquiry that all this is done; and done in so diligent and so prudent a manner? And that there is no need of any particular exhortations, instructions, or admonitions from us? Would to God there were any one congregation in the whole kingdom of which this might reasonably be presumed to be the case. But if it were indeed so, would not our concurrence with these wise and pious heads of families, in so good but so difficult a work, encourage and strengthen them to prosecute it with greater cheerfulness and vigour? Would it not quicken both their cares and their endeavours? And might it not, by the divine blessing, promote the success of them? Might it not gain on the minds of children and servants, to see that we did not think it beneath us, to care tenderly of their souls? And might not our tender and condescending regards to them in private, while it convinced them how well we meant them, render our public labours more acceptable and useful to them? Now we well know that the children and servants of the present

Excuses

generation are the hopes of the next, as they are probably those that in their turns will be parents and governors of families whose children and servants, when they arise, will one way or another feel the happy or unhappy consequences of our fidelity or neglect? And when such affairs are in question, shall we allow ourselves to plead,

See to the right use of time

We think that we have so much other business, and such various engagements of a different kind, that we cannot possibly attend to these things.

But give me leave, my brethren, to observe that the question here is not whether we can find out other agreeable ways of filling up our time? But whether those other ways are more important, and whether that different manner of employing it be more acceptable in the sight of God, and will turn to a better account in that great day when our conduct is to be finally reviewed by him? We must indeed have our seasons of recreation and our seasons of study, but it will easily appear that no regard to either of these will vindicate or excuse our neglect of the private duties we owe to our flock, in giving diligence to know their state (Prov. 27:23), and being careful to teach them, not only publicly but from house to house (Acts 20:20).

Neglecting the Souls of Men

Recreation, to be sure, can afford no just apology for neglecting the right use of time, since to follow this employment prudently might be made a kind of recreation from the labours of a sedentary and studious life. "A grave and severe recreation," you will perhaps say. Grave indeed I will acknowledge it to be, but not therefore to a serious mind less delightful. So much of those two noblest and sweetest exercises of the soul, devotion and benevolence, would naturally mingle with these pious cares and tender addresses, as would renew the strength which had been exhausted in our studious hours. And the manly, shall I say, or rather the godlike joy it would administer, would quite discountenance that which we find in the gay indulgences of a humorous and facetious conversation, though I see no necessity of forbidding that, at proper intervals, so far as its cheerfulness is consistent with wisdom and religion. And I am sure that if we can turn our seasons of recess from study to so profitable an account as would be answered by the duties which you know I have now in view, it will be a most happy art, well becoming one who is truly prudent, and would therefore husband his time to the best purposes for eternity. In which view it is evident that the smallest fragments of it, like the dust of gold or jewels, are too valuable to be lost.

Excuses

The great proportion of time to be given to our studies will no doubt be urged as a yet more material excuse. But here it is obvious to reply that a prudent care in the duties I am now recommending is very consistent with our employing a great deal of time in study; and particularly, with our giving it, what I hope we shall always learn to value and redeem, our morning hours, to which some of the evening may also be added. And if these will not generally suffice, give me leave to ask what are those important studies that would thus engross the whole of our time, excepting what is given to devotion and to what is generally called recreation?

I have had some little taste of the pleasures of literature myself and have some reason to hope, I shall not be suspected of any prejudice against it. Nor am I at all inclined to pass those contemptuous censures on the various branches of it, in which ignorance and sloth are often with strange stupidity, or with yet stranger assurance, seeking, and it may be finding, a refuge. But on such an occasion I must freely say I fear many things which employ a very large portion of our retired time, are studied rather as polite amusements to our own minds than as things which seem to have any apparent subserviency to the glory of God and the edification of our flock. And, consequently, I fear they will stand as articles of abatement, if I may so express it, in our final account. And when they come to be made manifest, will be sound works that shall be burnt, as being no better, in the divine esteem than wood, hay, and stubble (1 Cor. 3:12, 15), how beautifully soever they may have been varnished or gilded over.

3
Caution for Young Ministers

Let me here, in particular, address myself to my younger brethren with a frankness which may be to them more excusable, while I urge them to a Christian self-denial upon this head, where perhaps it may be of all others, the most difficult. I do not apprehend persons of your approved character to be in danger of any other kind of luxury and intemperance; but there is, if you will permit me so to call it, a sort of refined intellectual luxury with regard to which I am jealous over you, lest you should be seduced into it, or rather left some of you be already ensnared by its specious charms.

My young friends, I would not be so severe and cruel as to desire you should be confined from that high and elegant entertainment which a person of genius and taste will find in the masterly writings of the ancient orators, historians and poets. Nor would I confine you from those polite and elegant pieces, which our own, and other modern languages, may afford. From the wise man and the Christian you will learn many things of solid use, as well as matters of most delightful amusement. Neither would I pretend to forbid some mathematical and philosophical researches into which you are initiated in your academic course, and with which you will do well to retain and improve your acquaintance in the progress of life. These serve both to strengthen your rational faculties by that strenuous exercise and to improve your knowledge of the works of God, which will appear great, wonderful, and delightful in proportion to the degree of sagacity and diligence with which they may be searched out (Ps. 111:2). But it is one thing to taste of these poignant and luscious fruits, and another to feed and live upon them. One thing to make the most noble and substantial parts of them our entertainment and refreshment, and quite another to make their circumstantial curiosities the chief business of our study and the favorite subjects of our most attentive enquiry.

That true greatness and elevation of mind, which the Gospel is so admirably calculated to produce, would teach us a much more sublime science. And if for the sake of these little things, we neglect to pray for those whom God has committed to our care, to enquire into their religious state, and to pursue them with suitable applications and addresses, then the time will come when we shall assuredly own that we dearly purchased the most refined pleasures they could possibly give us. Not to say how much greater

Caution for Young Ministers

and nobler pleasure we even now resign while our duty is neglected. Oh, my brothers, let us consider how fast we are, as it were, posting through this dying life which God has assigned us, in which we are to manage concerns of infinite moment. How fast we are passing on to the immediate presence of our Lord, to give up our account to him. You must judge for yourselves; but permit me to say, that for my own part, I would not for ten thousand worlds be that man, who when God shall ask him at last how he has employed most of his time, while he continued a minister in his church, and had the care of souls, should be obliged to reply:

> Lord, I have restored many corrupted passages in the ancient classics, and illustrated many which were before obscure. I have cleared up many intricacies in chronology, or geography. I have solved many perplexed cases in algebra. I have refined on astronomical calculations; and left behind me many sheets on these curious and difficult subjects where the figures and characters are ranged with the greatest exactness and truth. And these are the employments in which my life has been worn out, while preparations for the pulpit, or ministrations in it, did not demand mine immediate attendance.

Oh, sires, as for the waters which are drawn from these springs, how sweetly they may taste to a curious mind that thirsts for them, or to an ambitious mind which thirsts for the applause they sometimes procure. I fear, there is often reason to pour them out before the Lord (2 Sam. 23:16–17), with rivers of penitential tears, as the blood of souls which have been forgotten while these trifles have been remembered and pursued.

On the best uses of labour

Since these papers have been prepared for the press, I have happily met with the Reverend Mr. William Leechman's excellent sermon on the temper, character, and duty of a minister of the gospel, preached before the Synod of Glasgow and Ayr, April 7, 1741 which, so far as I am capable of judging, on an attentive and repeated perusal, is one of the most masterly performances of the kind which ever fell into my hands. I am an entire stranger to the author but hope this sermon will meet with such just regard, as may encourage him to enrich our age and language with many other discourses in the spirit and manner, which he has there so admirably described and exemplified. As I am told, the below sermon was extorted from an excessive modesty, by the earnest importunity of his brethren. I am sure my reader will

Caution for Young Ministers

be pleased with the following specimen which I could wish deeply transcribed on every heart, and especially on my own.

> A just sense of the important relations we stand in to our respective flocks, and a genuine feeling of that tender affection which is due to them, won't allow us to hesitate one moment. Whether that part of our time is most worthily employed, which is taken up in doing real offices of friendship among them; or that part of it, which is spent in perusing the finest writings of the greatest genius that ever appeared in the world, or in polishing any little compositions of our own. Is the arranging of words, the beautifying of language, or even storing our own minds with the divinest sentiments, an employment of equal dignity and importance in itself, or equally pleasant on reflection, with that of composing differences, or extinguishing animosities, searching out modest and indigent merit and relieving it, comforting a melancholy heart, giving counsel to a perplexed mind, suspending pain by our sympathy and presence, though it were but for a moment, suggesting to an unfurnished mind proper materials for meditation in the time of distress, or laying hold of a favourable opportunity of conveying valuable instructions, and religious impressions, to a mind little susceptible of them on other occasions? There is

no need of saying anything in confirmation of this: It was the glorious character of Jesus, that he went about doing good.[13]

Preaching and ministry

Nor am I without my fears that a great deal of studious time is lost in an over artful composition of sermons, and in giving such polish and ornament as does not conduce to their usefulness nor any way balance the labour employed in the work. If we do not diligently watch over our hearts, this will be an incense offered to our own vanity, which will render our sacrifice less acceptable to God, however we and our hearers may be delighted with the perfume. Great plainness and simplicity of speech might often be more useful to the bulk of our auditory, and perhaps more acceptable too; on the whole, it might be at least equally beautiful. For all that are not children in understanding know that there is a natural and manly kind of eloquence, arising from a deep sense of the subject and an ardent love to the souls of our hearers, which is, of all others, the most to be desired and esteemed. And though such discourses may be attended with some little inaccuracies, and may want something of the varnish

---

[13] William Leechman, *The Temper, Character, and Duty of a Minister of the Gospel: A Sermon Preached Before the Synod of Glasgow and Air*, 2nd ed. (Glasgow: Robert and Andrew Foulis, 1741), 22-23.

which exacter preparation might set on, yet surely where a habit of speaking is formed by proper application, and the materials of a sermon are well digested in the mind, it will rise above a reasonable contempt. And if where exacter preparation is made, a care to reserve those niceties of composition deaden the manner of the delivery, and take off either its solemnity, its vigour, or its tenderness, I cannot but apprehend it as injurious to the character of the orator as to that of the Christian. The most celebrated speakers in judicial courts and in senates, have, in all nations and ages, pursued the method I now recommend; and the most acceptable preachers have successfully attempted it. On the whole, permit me to say, it would be a fatal thing to barter away the souls of our people for the highest and most just reputation of speaking well. Yet I fear there are many who in this view do it for nothing, and have not in any sense increased their wealth by the price (Ps. 44:12). But perhaps, after all, the most plausible excuse may be that which I have reserved for the last.

A necessary precaution of prudence
That the attempts I am proposing might displease those that attend upon our ministry; upon which account it may

seem, both with respect to them and ourselves, a necessary precaution of prudence to decline them.

This is the lion in the street (Prov. 26:13), which, as we are naturally too slothful, we often plead for staying within doors when our duty calls us abroad on these charitable errands. But I hope, on a nearer approach it will not be found so fierce, or so invincible, as a timorous imagination paints it.

I think, brothers, we make a very unfavourable representation of the tempter and character—not to say, of the breeding and understanding of our people—when we so readily take it for granted that they might be displeased with us for addressing those exhortations to them in private, which they seem so desirous of receiving from us in public. Let us ask our consciences, would they all be displeased? If not, the displeasure it might give to some can be no excuse for neglecting it with regard to others. And are we indeed so miserable as to be situated among whole congregations in whom ignorance, pride, and profaneness prevail to such a degree, that a minister, who would be welcome among them if he came only as a common visitant, should be looked upon with contempt or indignation, when he came expressly as a friend to their eternal interests, and would step a little out of the common way for their salvation? If this were really

Caution for Young Ministers

our case, who would not say with the prophet, "Oh that I had in the wilderness a lodging place of wayfaring men, though it were but such a wretched cave, as travelers find in a dessert, that I might leave my people, and go from them; for they be all an assembly of treacherous men!" Of treacherous men indeed (Jer. 9:2), yes; if, while they all themselves Christians and Protestants and profess to separate from their brethren on religious principles, they should think themselves injured and affronted by the exhortations of their ministers, while they would warn every man, and teach every man in all wisdom, that they might present them perfect in Christ (Col. 1:28).

But blessed be God, bad as the world is, there is no room to imagine this to be the case, or anything like it. Perhaps while we are delaying, and coldly deliberating about it, many lively Christians under our care are earnestly praying that God may put such a thing into our hearts. And should we attempt it, I doubt not, but they would receive us as an angel of God, or even as Christ himself (Gal. 4:14); then their love to us would be more abundantly confirmed, and their heart cemented in closer bonds than they have yet known. And many others would at least own that we acted in character, and maintained a more apparent consistency of behavior, if the affair were properly conducted.

The friend and the pastor

Did we indeed pretend to control them in the management of their temporal affairs, or to exercise a lordly dominion over their faith and their conscience, they might justly be displeased. Or did we craftily demand, that they should lay open to us the secrets of their breasts in confession, their suspicions were pardonable, and their resentments reasonable. But it must be great malice or folly to suspect any design of that infamous nature, from our vising them as pastors, with pious exhortations and affectionate prayers, as those who are concerned for them, and their children, and servants, that their souls may prosper and be in health (3 John 1:2). A solicitude for the health of their bodies is esteemed friendship and gratitude, and enquiries concerning it seem but common decency. And can it offend them to find we are solicitous about that welfare, which is infinitely more important and, by virtue of our office, our peculiar charge?

Yes, you will say, in one instance it will displease. When we are obliged to blame anything which we see amiss in them, then their pride will naturally take fire on such an occasion, and perhaps those whom we have thought our best friends will become our enemies, if we will venture to tell them such disagreeable truths (Gal. 4:16), as fidelity may

Caution for Young Ministers

extort in some circumstances. This is, after all, the main difficulty, and as I cannot wonder if it impresses our minds, I pray God to forgive the perverseness of those that make it so great. Yet, surely, it is possible to manage reproof so, as that in most instances, it shall oblige, rather than provoke. If we tell our hearers of their faults privately, if we do it with tenderness and respect and show by our manner of speaking that what we say proceeds from an humble fear—lest we should displease God, betray our trust, and injure their souls by the neglect. And if at the same time our behavior to them is, as it surely should be, constantly obliging to do our utmost to guard and shelter their character in the world, bad as the world is, then I believe few will quarrel with us; so long as truth and justice will permit us to bring our complaints of them to none but themselves. But we shall see, as Solomon observed, that he who rebukes a man will afterwards find more favour than he that flatters with his tongue (Prov. 28:23).

But supposing the worst that can happen, that folly and wickedness should prevail so far over all the tender and prudent addresses of the friend and the pastor as to render us evil for so great a good, and hatred for so generous, and so self-denying and instance of love, how could that hatred be expressed? Seldom in any more formidable manner than by withdrawing from our ministry, and discontinuing what they have done for our support, for the reviling of persons of such a character can seldom hurt any but themselves. Now I hope, brethren, we shall always retain so much of a manly, not to say a Christian spirit, as to choose to retrench some of our expenses, to forego some of the entertainments of life, to cast ourselves and families on providence, or even, it is were necessary, to subsist in an honest and creditable poverty by the daily labour of our own hands. That we shall do this much rather than meanly to crouch to such haughty sinners, and sacrifice duty, honour, and conscience, to the arrogance of their petulant temper. Let us fear God as we ought, and we shall find nothing to fear from them; but should be willing to imitate the fidelity and courage of the Baptist, though the wrath of a king might be provoked by it and imprisonment or martyrdom might be its reward.

I hope such considerations as these may effectually obviate the excuses, which indolence or cowardice may be ready to form, for our neglect of men's souls.

4

The Evils of Neglect

To consider the great evil of that neglect, as it appears in the sight of God, notwithstanding all these excuses, or any of the like kind with which we may endeavor to palliate it.

But who can fully represent it, as it appears to his capacious and all-penetrating view? What human mind can conceive the infinite evil? It is not, sirs, a subject on which to display the wantonness of wit, or the colourings of artificial harangue. A terrible kind of solemnity attends it, and I attempt the display of it with fear and trembling. If it seems a light matter to us to forbear to deliver those that in this sense are drawn unto death, and them that are thus ready to perish, then consider, my brethren, and oh may my own conscience always consider: what the death of the soul is, what gracious provision God has made to prevent it, and what peculiar obligations we are under—the labour to the utmost for the preservation of their lives.

What is the death of the soul?
Let us think, "what the death of the soul is." The apostle James intimates that it is a thought of great importance

when he says, "He that shall turn a sinner from the error of his way, shall save a could from death" (Jas. 5:20). As if he has said, "do but reflect what that is and you will find your success is its own reward." We well know that to save a soul from death is not merely to prevent the extinction of its being, though even that were much, but to prevent its positive, its lasting, its eternal misery. It is to prevent its being slain by the pointed and flaming sword of divine justice.

It is a tragic spectacle to behold a criminal dying by human laws, even where the methods of execution are gentle—as through the lenity of ours, they generally are gentler among us. And I doubt not, but it would grieve us to the heart to see any who had been under our ministerial care in that deplorable circumstance. But, oh, how much more deeply must it pierce our very souls to see them led forth to the last dreadful execution with those of whom Christ shall say, "As for these mine enemies, who would not that I should reign over them, bring them forth, and slay them before me!" (Luke 19:27). Oh how will it wound us to the beginning of those cries and wailings which must never end. How shall we endure reflection, "these wretches are perishing forever, in part because I would not take any pains to attempt their salvation!" And is this so strange a supposition that some once under our ministry may then perish in our sight? Would to God that it were less probable. On the contrary, let us consider

How many souls, precious and immortal as they are, seem to be continually dying around us?

Are there but few that miscarry? Let Peter inform us when he says that "the righteous are scarcely saved" (1 Pet. 4:18). Let our Lord himself inform us when he says, "Strait is the gate and narrow is the way that leads to life, and few there be that find it;" whereas "wide is the gather and broad is the way that leads to destruction, and many there be that go in" (Matt. 7:13–14).

We grieve to see epidemical distempers prevailing around us. We are ready, as providence call us, to visit the sick and the dying, and could take little pleasure in our own health if we did not endeavor to succor them as we have opportunity. But let us look around and see whether that distemper which threatens the death of souls, be not epidemical indeed. With all the allowances that charity can make, which "believe all things," and "hopes all things" (1 Cor. 13:7), which it can with a shadow of reason hope and believe, must we not own that there are marks of eternal death on many, and there are many more in whom we can see nothing which looks like a token of spiritual life? So that the best we can say of that is that there may be some latent sparks of it concealed in the heart which as yet produce effect to the honour of their profession or benefit of the world. In the meantime, sinners are spreading the infection of their infidelity, and their vices, far and wide. As if, like some illustrious wretches that have been miscalled heroes, they accounted the destruction of numbers their glory. Can we behold such a contagion spreading itself even in the Christian Church which ought to be healthful as the regions of paradise, and not bitterly lament it before God? Or can we seriously lament it, and not endeavor its redress?

What gracious provision God has made to prevent their death?

Is there not indeed "balm in Gilead? Is there not a physician there? (Jer. 8:22). Even this glorious gospel of the blessed God, whose efficacy we have so often heard of and seen? And shall they yet perish? Adored be the riches of divine grace, we know (and it is infinitely the most important part of all our knowledge) that there is a rich and free pardon proclaimed to all that will sue it out and accept the benefit in a proper, that is, in a grateful manner, for cordial acceptance and real gratitude is all it demands. One would expect the tidings should be as life to the dead. But we see how

Caution for Young Ministers

coldly they are received, how shamefully they are slighted, how generally, yea, how obstinately they are rejected. What is the consequence? Refusing to believe on the Son of God, "they shall not see life, but the wrath of God abides on them" (John 3:36), with an additional weight of vengeance, as it well may. Now is not this enough to make our very hearts bleed, to think that immortal souls should die under the gospel—die under aggravated guilt and ruin?

So that instead of being anything the better for this delightful message of peace and grace, they should be forever the worse for it and have reason to wish, throughout all eternity, they had never seen the faces, nor heard the voice of those that brought it, but had been numbered among the sinners of "Tyre and Sidon," of "Sodom and Gomorrah" (Matt. 10:15, 11:22).

If we do not, on the express authority of our Lord, believe this to be the case with regard to impenitent sinners under the gospel, we are not Christians of the lowest class. But if we do believe it, and are not affected with it, so far as to endeavor the recovery of sinners, I see not how any regard to our own temporal interest, or that of others, can entitle us to the character, either of prudence or humanity. This must be true, even if we had not been distinguished by a public office in the church, but had passed through life in the station of the obscurest among our hearers.

Obligation

We are under the peculiar obligation to endeavor the preservation of souls, not only in virtue of our experience as Christians, but of our office as ministers.

If we were only to consider our experience, as we are Christians, if we have anything more than the empty name, that consideration might certainly afford us a very tender argument, to awaken our compassion to the souls of others. We know what it is ourselves to be upon the brink of destruction, and in that sad circumstance to obtain mercy; and shall we not extend mercy to others? We have looked to Jesus, that we might live; and shall we not point him out to them? We have tasted that the Lord is gracious; and shall we not desire to communicate the same happy relish of his grace to all about us? He has magnified the riches of his pardoning love to us; and shall we not, with David, resolve, we will endeavour to teach transgressors his ways and labour to promote the conversion of sinners unto him (Ps. 41:13)? Even now is he keeping our souls: his visitation preserves our spirits (Job 10:12); and, as it is by his grace that we are what we are (1 Cor. 15:10), it is by having obtained help from

Caution for Young Ministers

him that we continue unto this day (Acts 26:22). And shall his grace daily bestowed upon us be in vain? And shall not we have compassion on our fellow-servants as our Lord continually has pity on us (Matt. 28:33)?

But our office, as ministers, completes the obligation, when we consider the view in which the Word of God represents that office, and the view in which we ourselves have received it.

As for the former of these, we are all acquainted with those representations; and it is greatly to be wished, for our own sake and that of our people, they may be very familiar to our minds. Let us often listen with becoming attention to the blessed God as speaking to us, in those words which he once addressed to the prophet Ezekiel, that faithful approved servant of the Lord:

> Son of man, I have made thee a watchman to the house of Israel; therefore hear the word at my mouth and give them warning from me. When I say to the wicked, thou shalt surely die; and thou givest him not warning, nor speakest to warn the wicked from his evil way to save his life; the same wicked man shall die in his iniquity, but his blood will I require at thine hand (Ezek. 3:17-18).

NEGLECTING THE SOULS OF MEN

And with apparent reason may the sentinel be punished for the desolation which the enemy makes, while instead of watching he sleeps.

We are elsewhere represented as men of God (1 Tim. 6:11), as soldiers of Jesus Christ (2 Tim. 2:3), as made overseers, or bishops, by the Holy Ghost (Acts 20:28), as under-shepherds in subordination to Christ, the great Shepherd and bishop of souls (1 Pet. 2:25). And ought not the thought, gentle as it is, to awaken us to a diligent inspection over the sheep he has committed to our care? Otherwise, we are but images of shepherds; as it is represented in those lively and awful words of God by Zechariah, which I think might strike terror and trembling into many, who in the eye of the world may seem the happiest of their brethren: "Woe to the idol shepherd, that leaveth the flock. The sword" of divine vengeance, which by his negligence he has justly incurred, "shall be upon his arm, and upon his right eye;" upon that eye, which should have watched over the flock, and that arm, which should have been stretched out for its rescue; so that he shall be deprived of those capacities he abused, and be made miserable in proportion to that abuse; for "his arm shall be clean dried up, and his right eye shall be utterly darkened" (Zech. 11:17).

Caution for Young Ministers

Such we know are the pathetic views, which the Scripture gives us of our office, and of the guilt and danger attending the neglect.

Remaining faithful to ordination vows
If my time would admit, I might farther urge the views with which we have ourselves received it, and engaged in it. Most of us, when we undertook the pastoral charge, solemnly recorded our vows before God: "that [we] would endeavour, with all diligence and zeal, to attend to the services of this body function; that we would 'be instant in season, and out of season' (2 Tim. 4:2), and labour to discharge the private, as well as public duties of the ministerial life." These vows of God are upon us, and every ordination of any of our brethren at which we assist, adds a farther and solemn obligation to them. Let us therefore take the greatest care that we do not deal deceitfully, and unfaithfully, both with God; and man. For it is most evident, that though the neglect of immortal souls is very criminal in every rational creature, it is most of all so in us, who have so deliberately, and so publicly, undertaken the charge of them.

It would indeed, in this case, not only be cruelty to them, but the basest treachery and ingratitude to our great Lord, who has lodged such a trust in our hands; a trust, which evidently lies so near his heart. Having redeemed his people with his own blood (Acts 20:28), he commits them to our care; and having acquired to himself the most tender claim to our love that can be imagined, he graciously requires this evidence of it, that we should feed his sheep, yes, his lambs (John 21:15-16). So putting our office in the most amiable and gentle view, and bringing in every sentiment of grateful friendship to excite our diligence in it.

However we may regard it, I do not doubt our blessed Redeemer considers it as the greatest favour and honour he could have conferred upon us. Upon being returned to his throne in the heavens, he chose us to negotiate his cause and interest on earth, and consigned to our immediate care that gospel he brought down from Heaven, as well as those souls which he died to save. He has made it the delightful labour of our life to follow him in his own profession and employment. He has made us to be, of all our fellow creatures, his most immediate representatives, and, in humble subordination to him, saviours of men. Does not the very mention of it cause our hearts to glow with a fervent desire, and generous ambition of answering so high a confidence? Could anyone of us endure the thought of betraying it?

In that case, how could we lift up our faces before him, when we shall, as we certainly must, see him eye to eye (Isa.

Caution for Young Ministers

52:8). Yes, my brethren, let us every hour recollect it. Our Master will, ever long, come, and reckon with us (Matt. 25:19). He will render to every man according to his works, as my text expresses it in exact harmony with the language of the New Testament (Matt. 26:27; Rom. 2:6; Rev. 22:12). And which of us would not then wish to appear before him as those that have been faithfully attached to his cause, and have distinguished themselves by a zeal for his service? Shall we then, any of us, repent of our activity in so good a work? Shall we wish that we had given more of our time to the pursuit of secular interest, or the curiosities of literature, and less to the immediate care of souls? Oh, my brethren, let us be wise in time. We have but one life to spend on earth, and that a very short one too. Let us make our best use of it, and lay it out in such kind of employments as we do verily believe will give us most satisfaction in the closing moments of it, and when eternity is opening upon us. It is easy to form plausible excuses for a different conduct, but our own hearts and consciences would answer us, if we would seriously ask them what the course of life in the ministerial office is, which will then afford the most comfortable review, and through the riches of divine grace the most pleasing prospect.

5
Applications and Practical Inferences

To the further application of these things, in some practical inferences from them. But what I have already said has been so copious, and so practical, as not to leave room to pursue such inferences at large.

The seriousness of ministry
You have all, I doubt not, prevented me in reflecting on the reason we have to humble ourselves deeply in the presence of the blessed God, while we remember our faults this day (Gen. 41:9). I do not, indeed, at all question, but that many of us have set before our people life and death (Deut. 30:15); and have, in our public addresses, urged their return to God by the various considerations of terror and of love, which the thunders of Mount Sinai, and the grace of Mount Zion, have taught us. We have, on great occasions, visited and entered into some serious discourse with them; and have often, I would hope, more or less daily, borne them on our hearts before God in our seasons of devout retirement. Blessed be God, that in these instances, we have, in any degree, approved ourselves faithful! It must give us pleasure

in the review. But, oh, why have not our prayers been more frequently presented, and more importunately enforced? Why have we not been more serious and more pressing in our private addresses to them, and more attentive in our contrivances to catch them in the net of the Gospel (Luke 5:10)? Let us ask our own consciences, this day, as in the presence of God, if there is no reason to apprehend that some who were once our hearers, and it may be our dear friends too, have perished through our neglect of souls. And of this neglect they are gone to eternal destruction for want of our more prudent, more affectionate, and more zealous care for their deliverance? In these instances, my brethren, though it is dreadful to say it and to think it, yet it is most certain that we have been, in part, accessory to their ruin. For this neglect we have reason to say, with trembling hearts, and with weeping eyes, deliver us from blood-guiltiness, from these unhappy souls, oh God of our salvation (Ps. 51:14)! And we have need with all possible earnestness to renew our application to the blood and righteousness of a redeemer, not daring to mention any services of our own as matter of confidence in his presence. How highly others may have esteemed them, who candidly look on the little we do, and perhaps make more charitable excuses for our

Applications

neglect, than we ourselves can dare to urge before God. Let remembrance of these things be for a lamentation.

Methods
Let us seriously consider what methods are to be taken to prevent such things for the time to come. They that have perished, have perished forever, and are far beyond the reach of our labours and prayers. But multitudes to this day surround us who stand exposed to the same danger and on the very brink of the same ruin. And besides these dying sinners, who are the objects worthy of most compassion, which the eye of man, or of God, beholds on this earth of ours. How many languishing Christians demand our assistance? Or, if they do not expressly demand it, appear so much the more to need it? Let us look round, my brethren, I will not say, upon the nation in general, but on the churches under our immediate care; and say, whether the face of them is such as becomes the societies of those whom the Son of God has redeemed with his own blood, and of those that call themselves the disciples, and members, of a once crucified and now glorified Jesus? Is their whole temper and conduct formed upon the model of his gospel? Are they such, as we would desire to present them before the presence of his glory? What is wanting cannot be numbered, and, perhaps,

we may be ready, too rashly, to conclude, that what is crooked cannot be made straight (Eccl. 1:15). Nevertheless, let us remember it is our duty to attempt it, as prudently as immediately, and as resolutely as we can. Many admirable advices for that purpose our fathers and brethren have given us; particularly Dr. Isaac Watts, in the first part of his humble attempt for the revival of religion, and Mr. David Some, in his sermon on the same subject: an excellent treatise, which reduced into practice would soon produce the noblest effects.[14]

Blessings in perseverance

That those important instruction may be revived and accommodated to present circumstances, with such additions as those circumstances require, we are, this day, having united our prayers to unite our counsels. I will not anticipate what I have to offer to your consideration in the more private conference on which we are quickly to enter. To form proper measures will be comparatively easy. To carry them strenuously into execution will be the great exercise of our wisdom and piety. May proportionable grace be given to animate us and to dispose them that are committed to our

---

[14] David Some, *The Methods to be Taken by Ministers for the Revival of Religion Consider'd, in a Discourse on Rev. 3:2* (London: Richard Hett, 1730).

Applications

care, to fall in with us in all our attempts for the honour of God and for their edification and comfort!

We shall esteem it, my friends, a very happy omen if your hearts be with ours on this occasion, and if you help forward so good and so necessary a design by your prayers to God for us. If you are sincere and affectionate in them, we may humbly hope that he, of whom we ask wisdom, will graciously impart it to us. May we assure ourselves that you will not only bear with us in the plainest addresses to you, which fidelity may oblige us to make, but will add all the weight of your countenance and interest to support us in our applications to others, whether public or private. And I have a cheerful confidence that all will not be in vain, but that he, who thus powerfully awakens our minds, will so succeed our labours that many whom we find under a sentence of condemnation, and ready to perish by it, will receive the forgiveness of their sins. That many will be recovered to a spiritual and divine life. And that many, as the happy consequence of all, will at length be fixed with us and with you in the regions of everlasting security and glory. Amen.

The EVIL *and* DANGER
OF
Neglecting the Souls of Men,

plainly and seriously represented

IN A

SERMON

Preach'd at

A MEETING of MINISTERS

At *Kettering* in *Northamptonshire*,
October 15, 1741.

And publish'd at Their REQUEST.

By *P. DODDRIDGE*, D.D.

Ουτος ο φοβων μεγιστος, ουτος ο κινδυνων εσχατος, περι τω
συνιεντι και τω κατορθεμενω το μεγεθ&, και της διαμαρτιας τον
ολεθρον.   Greg. Nazianz. *Orat. Apol.* §. 42.

L O N D O N,

Printed and sold by M. FENNER, at the *Turks-Head* in *Gracechurch-Street*.
MDCCXLII.

Scripture Index

Old Testament

Genesis
   8:21 23
   18:25 31
   20:6 27
   41:9 73
Exodus
   13:17 23
   23:4-5 26
Deuteronomy
   30:15 73
Joshua
   17:18 23
1 Samuel
   25:39 27
2 Samuel
   18:16 27
   23:5 23
   23:16–17 50
Job
   10:12 .... 30, 67
   16:6 27
   31:34 25
Psalms
   14:6 23
   25:11 23
   41:13 67
   44:12 53
   49:8 26
   51:14 74
   66:9 30
   82:2–4 24
   111:2 48
   133:1 21
Proverbs
   1:10–19 25
   3:29 25
   4:16–17 25
   6:12–14 25
   12:5–6 25
   17:15 25
   18:5 25
   21:7 25
   21:26 27
   21:28 25
   22:22–23 25
   23:10–11 25
   23:20–21 25
   24:12 23
   24:15 25
   24:23 25

24:11–12	19
26:13	54
27:17	21
27:23	44
28:15	25
28:17	25
28:23	58
29:4	25
29:10	25

Ecclesiastes

1:15	76
3:16–17	25
4:1–2	25
4:8	25
12:11	22

Isaiah

38:18–19	23
52:8	71
56:10–11	34

Jeremiah

8:22	64
9:2	55

Ezekiel

3:17–18	68
11:16	23
33:32	40

Habakkuk

3:17	23

Zechariah

11:17	69

Scripture Index

New Testament

Matthew
- 7:13–14 ... 63
- 10:11 ... 65
- 10:15 ... 65
- 23:23 ... 41
- 25:19 ... 71
- 26:27 ... 71
- 28:33 ... 67

Luke
- 5:10 ... 74
- 10:31 ... 30
- 19:27 ... 62

John
- 3:36 ... 65
- 21:15–6 ... 70

Acts
- 20:20 ... 44
- 20:28 ... 68, 70
- 26:22 ... 67

Romans
- 2:6 ... 71

1 Corinthians
- 3:12 ... 46
- 3:15 ... 46
- 4:3–4 ... 29
- 13:1 ... 40
- 13:7 ... 63
- 15:10 ... 67

Galatians
- 4:14 ... 55
- 4:16 ... 57

Colossians
- 1:28 ... 55

1 Timothy
- 6:11 ... 68

2 Timothy
- 2:3 ... 68
- 3:17 ... 34
- 4:2 ... 69

James
- 5:20 ... 62

1 Peter
- 2:25 ... 68
- 4:18 ... 63

3 John
- 1:2 ... 56

Revelation
- 3:2 ... 76
- 22:12 ... 71

Date Completed	Name

H&E *Publishing*

WWW.HESEDANDEMET.COM

www.ingramcontent.com/pod-product-compliance
Lightning Source LLC
Chambersburg PA
CBHW030914080526
44589CB00010B/296